GOLF

The Rhyme and Reason

A Light-hearted Look
At The Mysteries of Golf

By Freddie Mitman
with cartoons by Robert Duncan

FastPrint Publishing

http://www.fast-print.net/bookshop

GOLF: THE RHYME AND REASON

A catalogue record for this book is available from the British Library

ISBN 978-178456-431-5
(Also available as a hardback: ISBN 978-178456-409-4)

First published 2016 by
FASTPRINT PUBLISHING
Peterborough, England.

ABOUT THE AUTHOR

Freddie Mitman began his working life as a farm manager, but says that after a year he found that things were not going fast enough for him. He then joined the world of sales and worked in London on various projects until starting his own sales company. In an active commercial life he has built two international companies.

During this time he has given over 1,500 motivational and aspirational presentations in the UK, the USA and mainland Europe.

He has had a book on positive attitude of mind published, and also a Christmas book for all who still believe in Father Christmas, both children and adults.

His love affair with golf started when he gave up playing hockey at the age of 35.

His love for the game has not diminished over the years, although time has allowed him to be only a weekend golfer.

His handicap has been as low as five at its best, and has passed through, and revisited, various stages of hopelessness along the way.

He fully understands the highlights, the horrors and the humour that, together, make this game so intriguing.

PREFACE

Golf is a wonderful game.

To whatever level our game has risen or sunk, there are moments of great enjoyment in every round, as well as a few of frustration.

We golfers always live in hope, as we make our swings, that we will hit that great shot we all know lies within us.

Often we don't, but we still hope!

You will note that the illustrations depict male golfers. This book equally applies to male or female golfers.

We had thought of having some ladies in the visuals but felt that, whichever section we might have chosen, it could have indicated the topic applied particularly to ladies. We did not want to venture down this road, so kept the illustrations all male. Safer we thought!

Before, after, and during each golf game our minds run the full gambit of emotions, from euphoric to suicidal, but still, at the next opportunity, we are back on the course trying again.

We golfers relax in our chairs, lie in bed, sit in aircraft or cars, or even at the office, imagining the great games to come, even playing particular courses in our imagination, the way we know we can, or should be able to play.

The great majority of golfers will never break 100. To some this would be the height of achievement, but things keep conspiring to hold us back just when we feel we have this game almost mastered.

This is a book of golfing thoughts. We all have them.

The book will probably mirror some of your own thoughts, past or present.

It will not teach you how to be a better golfer. I will leave that to the technical experts. It will not teach you to be a winner more often. I leave this to fate, belief, practice, and perhaps the failings of your opponent!

It will, however, help you to smile with me at the many angels and demons that accompany us as we play the game, or think about the game.

I have used verse to capture each pattern of thought, and have given a short introduction to each section so you know what the verse is going to be about, so that you can avoid any section that may cause undue horrors for you.

I first fell in love with golf when I was in my thirties and still playing more active sports. The love affair progressed to the exclusion of all other sports activities.

Golf is one of the few games where we have to take the blame, or the accolade, for all the shots we make.

The ball lies exactly where we have hit it. The green is not going to move, or a barrier suddenly be placed between us and it. We will have worked out the distance and allowed for any wind. We have chosen which club to use. When we hit that ball, where it finishes is entirely our fault, and we alone have to take all responsibility.

In tennis we can blame the topspin our opponent cleverly placed on the ball; in snooker, and even bowls, we have to navigate through obstacles placed by others in our way.

In rugby or football or hockey we could be starved of access to the ball.

Golf is like an exacting mistress who wants our entire concentration and affection, and can bring us great joy or frustration, or even misery if we don't treat her with the respect she believes she is due.

With weekend, or even very occasional, golfers, the game is never far from our thoughts. We even measure some distances in golf shots. 100 yards becomes a wedge shot, or 9, 8 or 7-iron depending upon the state of our game at the time. 500 yards becomes a par 5 that professionals might enjoy.

For me, I only hit golf balls in feet and yards; that was the way golf was supposed to be. Where proper distances have been converted into metres, I convert them back into yards before playing my shot.

In this book we will share thoughts on most aspects of our game, including The Dreaded Slice, The Horrendous Hook, Bunkers and Other Fiendish Obstacles, The Rough, The Shot That Brings Us Back, The Shout of 'Fore', Golf Attire, Magazines, Golf Shops, and many other inspiring or frightening thoughts and actions that make up our favourite game. We will also take a view from the 19th hole.

I am looking out of the window now and the rain is lashing down out of a leaden sky. I'm still going to play golf this afternoon because I just know that the odd bright period the forecasters promised will arrive at the course just as I pull into the car park.

In fact there is a lighter shade of grey passing overhead right now and it's heading roughly in the right direction.

It's going to be a great afternoon...

SWING THOUGHTS

During our golfing life our minds have absorbed, or partly absorbed, a myriad of advice from professionals, instruction manuals, or helpful playing partners.

The advice is always well meant, and mostly correct.

The problem is remembering it all in the couple of seconds we take to make our swing.

Somehow our mind can be so overfilled with good advice it doesn't know which piece to enact at which moment.

To make things worse we have read, or have been advised of, many different solutions to any problem with which we are currently afflicted.

These all have to be sorted, remembered, or rejected during that couple of seconds. No wonder we sometimes don't make that perfect swing.

We're told that once we get it right, and it becomes automatic, then things get easier. I'm still waiting.

Of course, we don't see our own swing in action, but others do.

Our helpful playing partners might give us advice at one of those moments when we're approaching suicide, but that only gives one more, sometimes doubtful, item to add to our already clogged golfing brains.

The following verse lists some of them.

Swing Thoughts

My stance must be square
And be checked with great care,
With grip not too tight
I'll imagine the flight.
Transferring my weight
Keep my left arm quite straight.
Unlocking my knees
Sweep those woods off the tees.
Hit irons down through
Strike the ball fair and true.
Must keep my head still
Turn my shoulders at will,
And then, standing tall,
Swing the club through the ball.
My nerves I must soothe
So I keep my swing smooth,

Then follow through clean
So I'm facing the green.
These things I must do
So the ball will fly true.
But try as I might
I just can't get it right,
While I'm in full swing-
Can't remember a thing.
I'm just on the brink
Of restoring to drink,
My brain cannot cope –
So I'll just hit and hope.

SWING SPEEDS

A lot of golf shops now have computers in their practice bays that can measure our swing speed.

It is a bit demoralizing at first to find that our swing speed is only half that of a tour professional.

No wonder they hit the ball further.

But they are younger and fitter than we are, and have bodies that bend and twist in a way that ours seems unable to duplicate.

They, of course, hit hundreds of balls each day in practice; we don't have the time other than those precious hours we dedicate to actually playing the game.

The correct shaft in our clubs can help this situation, we're told.

On deeper investigation we find that we're currently using the wrong clubs, with the wrong shafts.

The shops, of course, have a solution for this.

It is possible to buy a swing-speed monitor that you can practise with at home. However, because of constant reminders of the inadequacy of our own swing speed, we tend to make appointments that our bodies can no longer, or perhaps were never able to keep. This can become a danger to our scorecards, and our backs, and perhaps even our playing partners, by trying to emulate the swing speeds of our golfing heroes.

Swing Speeds

Our swing speed can be monitored
To give golf shops some clues
Of types of shaft our clubs might need,
And what balls we should use.

The flaw in all these measurements
Is that in practice we'll
Not always be consistent, it
Depends on how we feel.

The pressures in our workplace or
Some aches and pains that may
Just change the way we swing the club,
It's not the same each day.

When we have had a rough night, or
Have fought a traffic jam,
We'll hit it like a tiger or
Just waft it like a lamb.

Our swing speed won't be relevant,
It matters not one jot –
Let's keep things as they are and use
The clubs that we have got.

THE SLICE

This chapter is for the golfer who is still under the hypnotic power of a persistent slice.

Some of us get through this stage in our golfing careers, some never.

To many golfers, hitting across the ball is as natural as breathing.

Avid 'slicers' who have not, at some stage, been dragged away by people in white coats have learned to live with the shape of this shot. Some manage temporarily to temper its excesses. However they know, deep down, like an alcoholic, that just one wayward shot could herald another period of persistent trouble, searching for the ball in the rough, or the woods, or the out of bounds, that lie along the right-hand side of the fairway. For left-handed golfers this is, of course, the left-hand side.

Even if we are one of those rare players who now hit it straight, this verse will remind us of troubled times when we were 'sliceaholics', and we can smile at the memories and be proud we conquered the habit - almost, anyway.

The Slice

My golf is played with verve and zest;
I always try to do my best.
This game would be just paradise
If only I could cure my slice.

I've been to experts round the world;
Their special cures were all unfurled.
They said they'd fix it in a trice,
But still I had this dreadful slice.

Thought patterns for my swing they gave;
They told me all the shots I'd save.
Although they all seemed very nice,
Not one of them could cure my slice.

I read the magazines and books,
I learned the swing that causes hooks,
My friends all gave me their advice,
But somehow, still, I've got this slice.

I bought a club with off-set head,
To banish all my slicer's dread;
The golf shop said they'd guarantee
My future game would be 'slice-free'.

I took it proudly to the course,
My swing was smooth, I used no force;
I hit that ball with balanced ease -
It curved right, deep into the trees.

The club on which my hopes had clung,
Now sits up in my loft, among
The other clubs that didn't work,
But still displays its off-set quirk.

My playing partners don't hit straight,
They hit it early, hit it late.
The ball goes left, right, high or low,
They're never sure where it will go.

I know just where my ball will go,
The pathway of its flight I know.
Consistency is what I've got,
I don't have any other shot.

I now stand facing left off tee,
I know the shape my shot will be;
I hit it left, with steely nerve,
And then just watch its graceful curve.

And where the ball has ended it
Is just where I intended it;
No longer do I fight my slice,
It's now my virtue, not my vice.

THE HOOK

In the innocence of my pre-golf life I saw a hook as something you nailed to a wall to hang pictures from, or put on the end of a line for fishing purposes. As a child I remember I was very scared of Captain Hook, in *Peter Pan*. I learned, also, that it could be a projecting piece of land (I understand that Holland has one).

The saying 'by hook or by crook', meaning by fair means or foul, creeps into many conversations, and can also apply to some golfers' tactics.

It also represented something I often tried to get off, when I might have done something wrong.

It was, however, when I started to play golf that I learned its true meaning.

A hook is, of course, the shot, especially off the tee, that develops a strong will of its own and curves to the left quite uncontrollably, or to the right if you are left-handed.

It became my bête noire and lost me a great number of golf balls in my early playing days.

I have great affinity with those who suffer from the hooking disease, and hope they can find periods of hook-free Utopia. Perhaps even with the help of professional guidance they can find that particular antibiotic that can cure the symptoms of their particular affliction.

The Hook

The ball swings gently right to left;
You've hit a draw, a worthy shot.
But if you overdo this trend,
The dreaded hook is what you've got.

A fade, or even slice, we hear,
Will listen when you talk to it.
The hooked shot is completely deaf -
It takes no notice, not one bit.

A lesser evil than the slice,
Which some can conquer or abate,
That they can quell for quite a spell,
But never quite eradicate.

The curving path of vicious hooks,
A hooker's curse that's rarely tamed,
Can travel several fairways to
The left of where you thought you aimed.

A hook is like a nasty spell,
An intermittent evil curse;
It can't be cured by facing right,
That only seems to make it worse.

When hooking gets you in its grip,
A habit that you can't rebut,
It can affect most any club
And some can even hook a putt!

But as it came, it often goes,
And then once more your game stands tall.
You hit again your gentle fade
That is the envy of us all.

THE SHOT THAT BRINGS US BACK

In every round we play there is a mixture of very good shots, not-so-good shots, and terrible shots.

A great professional golfer once stated that he will make six bad shots in a round. So when he makes one of his six he is not demoralized, for he knows he will repair the damage with a birdie or an eagle and anyway, that is just one of the six bad shots he will make in that round.

We weekend golfers are somewhat different. The number of bad shots we will make far exceeds six. Just how far, we will not go into detail now. We more likely think that we will play only six very good, or bordering on very good, shots in the forthcoming round.

Now it can happen that one of our six is so good that it is almost unbelievable - prodigious distance, perfectly judged, exactly as we would imagine perfection to be.

We've done it.

We have proved we have one shot in our armoury that is the equal of anybody's. Wow! We get to thinking that perhaps we could do it again and again - a dangerous thought.

This one great shot will bring us back on to the course in spite of the fact that the rest of the round was so bad that we were considering, for the moment, that we might have to give the game up. We will hang on to that shot like a life-raft.

The Shot That Brings Us Back

Now every golfer has a slump,
However good we are;
Play shots that make us feel a chump,
That don't go straight or far.

We think we've lost the golfing plot,
Our game is on the rack,
And then we hit that perfect shot –
The shot that brings us back.

That shot will somehow save the day,
We've rarely hit the like.
Those bad shots seem to fade away
Beside that perfect strike.

We knew when we had hit that shot,
Our swing had been sublime.
We'd proved that we could do it once –
So why not every time?

Those quitting thoughts we won't retain;
Give golf another crack.
Perhaps we'll play that shot again,
The shot that brings us back.

ONE GREAT ROUND

Sometimes our game comes together. We play good shots not just singly, but in clusters. Luck seems to favour the bounce of our ball, trees don't get in the way, and the flags are set close to where our ball lands!

When one of these rare occasions occurs it boosts our confidence no end, and we just can't wait for the next round.

With the memory of the scintillating game we've just played fresh in our minds, our confidence is on a high.

We smile knowingly at our golfing partners on the weekend, but we refrain from telling them about the wonderful round we've just completed. We want to surprise them!

We often do, but not the way we have envisaged. Golfing fate seems to want to return our overall game back to normality; it wants to invoke the law of averages.

The brilliance of the game before just fades into a happy memory. The skills we showed that last time out seem to have left us.

It is possible, of course, to have two great rounds running, but it is very rare. If ever we do, we take a step closer to Utopia. There are some dangers, of course. If we put in a card for these great rounds, we pay in the future by having to play off a lower handicap!

One Great Round

Last week I joined a golfing group
And, though it may seem weird,
Quite suddenly, from nowhere, some
Consistently appeared.

My confidence grew steadily,
My golf showed signs of flair;
Instead of being regular,
Mistakes became quite rare.

The round was great, I won the day;
Somehow I couldn't fail.
I foolishly imagined that
I'd found golf's Holy Grail.

I brought my new-found confidence
To my next weekend round.
I longed to introduce to all
The 'new me' that I'd found.

But somehow all the magic which
Surrounded me that day,
Had disappeared like early snow
That quickly melts away.

My game returned to normal, with
Its wildly wayward trends.
I was a little thankful that
I hadn't told my friends.

They say that just one swallow will
A summer never make.
That we can't always play our best
Is sometimes hard to take.

BUNKERS

I wonder who invented bunkers, or sand traps, as they are sometimes called?

Perhaps a course by the seaside was bordered by sand and some disillusioned golfers had fun trying to hit the ball from the sand, and decided that that fun could be enjoyed by players on inland courses as well.

Whatever happened, leading golfers must have decided that the game of golf was too easy and, to make it more difficult, they invented the bunker.

Bunkers have now grown like a disease, disfiguring courses around the world. Some courses have the disease badly, with deeper and wider infections. Some, on the other hand, have only occasional blemishes.

The career of course-designing is often taken up by professional golfers to whom difficulty is an exciting challenge. It may be exciting for them but, for we weekend golfers, the fewer difficulties built into a course the better.

The bunker, and how to avoid it, and how to get out of it, has become part of the modern game, and we must accept this hazard as part of our golfing life.

Bunkers

Now bunkers can look very grand
With sunlight glinting off the sand;
But they are placed with fiendish art,
Designed to break a golfer's heart.

The 'pros' seem pleased if they roll in -
Just splash it out beside the pin.
We weekend golfers fret about
The shots we'll take to get it out.

We try by any means on earth
To give those traps the widest berth,
But course designers find a way
To bring those bunkers in to play.

When faced with a protected green,
With bunkers littered round the scene,
We choose a line that's 'bunker-free',
The safest route that we can see.

We're sure, by its projected flight
Our ball will miss it on the right.
That clear path to the green we see –
Is not what it pretends to be.

The ground is sculptured with such skill
The ball is drawn, against its will,
Through valleys, mounds, and gentle slopes
That are designed to thwart our hopes.

Those hills and valleys guide our ball
To where it shouldn't be at all.
Instead of sailing through the gap,
It ends up in that sandy trap.

But we will always find a way
To get it out, continue play;
Just one more hazard there to bear –
But wish they'd dug the thing elsewhere.

THE ROUGH

Some time ago, friends of mine and I decided to enter ourselves as a team into a well-known local competition.

We had to think of a team name, under which our team would be known. There were many company names, or attempts at humorous names, already entered.

We gave some serious thought, over a few beers after our Saturday morning game, and got to talking about the round we had just completed.

The rough was, at that time, fairly high, and most of us had spent the majority of the round hacking our way out of it. We decided that, as we loved the game of golf, we must learn to love the rough as well.

We should be delighted for our ball to have landed anywhere on the course at all, even in the rough.

We, therefore, in this positive mood, chose 'The Rough Lovers' as our team name.

Now, however innocently one might choose a name, innuendo can always raise its head in the minds of some.

Although our name was reluctantly accepted, it seemed to create some embarrassment within the committee running the competition. Because of our attitude to the rough, which was in abundance on that particular course, we actually won the competition!

At the presentation of the cup our name was not mentioned, neither was it engraved on the cup among the historical winners. We have not played under that particular name since, as we do not wish to stimulate the sensibilities of minds that are not as pure as our own!

Loving being in the rough is still part of our individual codes, and I'm sure this helps us play our shots from this loving environment.

The Rough

The fairway can be hard to hit,
With hills, or slopes, where balls can't sit;
And, if those hazards aren't enough,
It's bordered by a thing called rough.

The rough is nature's habitat -
Uneven ground that's rarely flat.
The grass is left to grow its best,
Where rabbits hide, and birds can nest.

We aim at fairways – but can miss;
Although it won't be quite death's kiss,
The penalty is very tough.
For now we're in that dreaded rough.

And when we try to hit the ball
From grass that has become quite tall,
The grass just wraps around the head
And seems to stop our swing stone dead.

Then when, at last, we hit it right,
We cannot quite control the flight;
It sails across the fairway wide
Into the rough the other side.

Some players go from rough to rough
As if they like that tangled stuff
Where nature draws them, when it calls.
To compensate, they find lost balls!

So when we're in that rough we love,
We look for guidance from above;
Hit through that ball with all our might,
Just hoping we will get it right.

GOLF BALL MAGIC

The golf game is built around the golf ball and the quality of its journey from tee to hole.

Golf ball manufacturers are numerous and, to capture us as customers they need to extol the special virtues of their ball versus others.

This only really matters to the top ten percent of golfers.

The vast majority of golfers don't really need the special features that give extra distance.

They know, in their hearts, that hitting the green in the regulation number of shots will be a rare occurrence anyway, so why spend a lot of money missing it?

The features of the golf ball that aid shaping the shot, or creating back-spin on the green, are only useful to the better golfer.

To most average golfers the shape of the shot is in the hands of fate, and they have never ever had a ball spin back on a green!

They do sometimes buy new balls, in pristine new packets, from golf shops and pro shops, but have an eye more on the price than on the characteristics of the ball. At Christmas time, gifts of packets of golf balls can be gratefully received. Unfortunately, the joy of hitting a shining new golf ball does not last very long.

This investment in golf balls is subsidized by finding lost balls. Playing with these teaches us the skill of adapting to any ball.

Losing expensive balls can be very costly. I played with a stranger recently who bought a plastic bag of ten golf balls at the club pro shop. On the eleventh hole he had to borrow some more from me!

However, he seemed to thoroughly enjoy the game and celebrated copiously in the bar afterwards.

Golf Ball Magic

Golf balls are sold in billions,
With many makes to choose;
Some golfers are particular
About the ones they use.

They come in boxes giving all
Statistics of their flight,
But somehow they're assuming that
We'll always hit it right.

Spin factors, dimple numbers, all
Are there for us to read;
Compression ratios and such -
More facts than we will need.

Not all golf balls are white, we find,
So many colours seen;
But even for the Irish, they
Don't make a ball in green!

And then we can buy golf balls cheap
Of some quite obscure make.
And even low-priced 'lake balls' that
Have never seen a lake.

Some golfers play with balls they've found,
That others hit, and lost.
When playing with those pick-ups we
Don't need to count the cost.

A note to those who find lost balls
As round the course they stroll -
A golf ball's never truly lost
Until it's ceased to roll.

Whatever ball is on our tee
As we commence our round,
Our only thought is 'hit the thing'
And hope it can be found.

THE RIGHT SPHERE

A golf ball is quite small and it sits upon an enormous sphere of 25,000 miles in circumference.

An error some of we golfers make is to hit the wrong sphere first.

We can spot the golfers with this affliction when we follow them around the course.

We can see a row of divots, not very far apart and not necessarily in a straight line, disappearing into a wood or thicket from which strange golfing oaths are emanating.

This condition can be easily cured. It is only practice, a perfect stance, being exactly the right distance from the ball, the correct swing path, keeping the head very still, and the knees bent to the right angle; easy, really.

I can't see how golfers can consistently be troubled by this problem. But some do find it possible.

One could suggest practice swings as a cure, but then there might well be clusters of divots instead of single ones. Perhaps not such a good idea.

The Right Sphere

Just one point six eight inches is
A golf ball's known diameter;
It's just the same when hit by a
Professional or amateur.

It sits upon a larger sphere
Of many thousand miles around –
Amid the beauties of the course
Our golf ball lies there on the ground.

To make the game enjoyable,
We must remember what to do -
Just line up square, and swing our club
And hit the smaller of the two!

THE RAINY DAY

We play our golf in all sorts of conditions.

Rain, wind, fog, heat waves, frost, and even snow before it is thick enough to close the course.

Why do we persist in conditions not conducive to playing good golf?!

Firstly, we do not all play good golf anyway. Adverse weather conditions can often give us something extra to blame!

Secondly, when we have arranged a game, sometimes in a very busy schedule of other activities, such as work, we feel we must give it a chance, whatever the forecast weather conditions. Also we must never let our playing partners down by not turning up, for they too have fitted the round into their own busy schedules.

When we take a count of the days that we have been rained off completely in the past year or so, and realize it is only a small percentage, we therefore trust the law of averages to create that unexpected bright period.

When the forecast is for rain, heavy at times, and some bright periods, my tendency towards positive thinking leads me to believe that I will be playing in a bright period. Others may warn me that I will get soaking wet. They can be right, of course, but why should my excitement be tempered by such negative thoughts? I have waterproofs, don't I?

The Rainy Day

I climbed into my car with hope
And set out for the course;
I hadn't driven far before
The rain increased in force.

With windscreen wipers working hard,
Drove through that heavy squall.
With such torrential rain, I thought
There's not much more to fall.

The forecast was not positive,
They'd threatened general rain;
I still drove toward the club with hope –
My wife thinks I'm insane.

Bad forecasts can deceive and make
You change the plans you've made.
I never quite believe that it
Will rain on my parade.

My partners stare up at the sky
In hopes we might still play,
Their optimism searching for
A patch of lighter grey.

"Come on; let's wait no more, the rain
Is falling with less force,
And start our round before some fool
Decides to close the course."

We walked together to the tee,
Those stormy clouds defied;
By challenging the elements
We felt a surge of pride.

We did not play that well, it was
So wet we could have swum.
But you can never tell when that
Bright period will come.

The rain, of course, it never stopped,
It grew as black as night;
With fairways almost waterlogged –
We carried on in spite.

I left the 18th green and put
My rain gear in the car,
Ran from that washed-out scene
And met the others in the bar.

Today has been our gain, we all
Surmised as we dried out.
The fairways needed rain, for they
Have suffered in the drought.

The sunshine's on the way, the rain
Today was just a freak.
The course will play so well, when we
All meet again next week.

FORE

On a normally peaceful golf course, amid the quiet bird-song and the buzzing of summer bees there is suddenly heard a fearsome cry of FORE!

This, we have learned, is a warning that a golfer somewhere has hit a ball off its intended line and fears it may hit somebody on another part of the course.

Those of us hearing the warning shout now have to make some instant calculations.

1. Was it us they were trying to warn?
2. From which direction may the missile be coming?
3. When they say 'Fore Left', am I left or right of the launching site?
4. Is the ball coming from on high, or is it travelling with great force at head height?

5. Should I stand bravely and ignore it?
6. Should I dive for cover?

We have only a very few seconds to answer all these questions, so there is no time for deliberation or discussion.

A few seconds later we are safe to continue our game, but may have to wait a bit until our heart rate has returned to normal.

Fore!

'Fore left' is shouted
Loud and clear
A warning call for
All to hear.

Now am left? Or
Am I right?
And what's the angle
Of its flight?

What is that missile's
Closing rate?
Am I about to
Meet my fate?

The shout was urgent,
I can bet
It's coming like an
Exocet!

The clock has ticked, the
Time has passed;
Can breathe again, I'm
Safe at last.

GOLFING MAGAZINES

On almost all bookshelves at airports, railway stations and newsagents our eyes are somehow drawn to the covers of the latest golf magazines. They are on the lower shelves!

Pictures of our favourite professional golfers performing exquisite shots tempt us to buy the magazine, in the forlorn hope that in it we will find that missing chord in the symphony of our own golf game.

If we have some reading time to spare, or we are on a long journey somewhere, we can avidly absorb all the knowledge and advice within its covers.

Although we can't always be playing the game we love, at these times the magazine welcomes us with open arms into the world we are missing.

It all seems so easy in the pictures we study, that we can almost see ourselves achieving that 'follow through' position, or duplicating that balanced back swing so beautifully displayed.

We learn the distance certain clubs should go and wonder why our own don't go nearly that far, but are encouraged by the advertisement on the next page for clubs that give us 'that extra distance'.

We enjoy the magazines and live, for a period, in the euphoria of hope that the magic displayed in these magazines could somehow attach itself to us.

Golfing Magazines

At times when circumstance conspires
To keep off those rolling greens,
We put out those withdrawal fires
By buying golfing magazines.

To stop the shots that spoil our cards,
The experts give the 'whys' and 'whats'
Of how to gain those extra yards,
And trim our score by lots of shots.

Our putting stance and grip was wrong;
By changing it we have the means
Of sinking putts, both short and long,
And saving strokes on all the greens.

Advertisements for clubs we read,
That, purely by their new design
Will give us all the help we need
To strike it on the perfect line.

If we add all the shots we'll save
By putting straight, and hitting far,
The skills we've learned will surely pave
The way to playing under par.

But now we're back upon the course
Our new-found skills seem all in vain;
In fact they've made our scoring worse
By muddling our golfing brain.

MOBILE PHONES

It would seem that everyone today carries a mobile phone.

These phones cry for attention and their owners have to pick them up and soothe them, as one would a child.

It would seem that being separated from these phones is like an umbilical cord has been cut and life can't continue without it.

Mobile phones are, of course, very important in the right place, at the right time. Business, as it is enacted today, has reached a pace that makes communication by mobile phone essential. Family communication is kept alive by mobile phone contact.

However, there must be places where they are not permitted to cry for attention. These include churches, theatres, cinemas, public libraries and other places where concentration must never be disturbed. Golf courses are among these.

The only urgent matter needing attention on the golf course or in the clubhouse is golf itself.

Mobile Phones

Most golf clubs have a stringent rule:
All mobile phones are banned,
And woe betide the golfer who
Is found with one in hand.

There are some 'phoneaholics' who
***Must** bring it when they play,*
*And any noise it makes just **must***
Be answered straight away.

To confiscate the phone would be
A tragedy, you'd think,
As bad as if you would deny
An alcoholic, drink.

A golf course is a place of peace
With cares, and noise dispelled,
Where minds stay focused on the game
And sportsmanship upheld.

Golf partners keep quite quiet and
From any noise desist,
Before they say 'bad luck' and such,
When little putts are missed.

The concentration needed for
A perfect swing, we've found,
Requires that depth of quiet where
There's not a single sound.

Complaints have been recorded and
Some golfers have avowed
That butterflies can even beat
Their wings a bit too loud.

And even in the clubhouse there's
A ban on mobile phones,
So peace cannot be shattered by
Obnoxious ringing tones.

And also in the members' bar
Are those who will resent
The clicking noise of prodding,
As text messages are sent.

Nor do the members wish to hear
The details and the woes
Of family complications and
Domestic tos and fros.

So phones are left in owners' cars -
Some addicts shed a tear -
Those cars make many ringing sounds –
But nobody can hear.

GOLF ATTIRE

Only on club outings, or the Ryder Cup, do golfers dress in unison.

We wear items in which we are comfortable, and which wash well.

Golf can be a muddy business from time to time and it can splash quite liberally over anything we're wearing.

Being slightly overweight makes comfort my main concern, knowing that creating a suave and debonair impression is unlikely, whatever I wear.

Some, however, achieve this even on a Saturday morning in high winds and rain. I must work on it!

Keeping warm and dry in winter can be a problem because, with many sweaters and a waterproof jacket on, we become unable to bend athletically, and our game suffers. We play anyway because we are all in the same boat metaphorically, I hope, anyway.

Keeping cool in summer is easier and the game is far more enjoyable with a little warmth, and we even enjoy the sun on our backs on some days. I wish, however, that we actually played that much better when the conditions were good.

Headgear varies from balaclavas to bobble hats, and golf hats advertising certain clubs, balls, hotels and companies.

Extra-warm gloves are carried in winter so that our hands do not freeze between shots. For some even, these must be colour-coordinated.

Golf Attire

Now have you ever noticed, few
Men golfers dress the same?
Some have that Gatsby elegance,
Some put all style to shame.

I've worked out now the reason why
Some wear mismatching clothes;
They had no fashion expert there
To guide them as they chose.

They'd just picked up the things that were
Most comfortable to wear;
Their clothes might clash a bit, but then,
They didn't really care.

If they'd put on some stylish clothes,
On these their mind might dwell.
In trying to protect them, they
Might not have played so well.

The golfing sweater they had worn
In many hard-fought matches,
Still keeps them warm, although it had
Acquired some holes and patches.

Their trousers had a few small tears
Through catching on some thorn,
But they were very comfortable,
The best they'd ever worn.

The purpose for them going to
The golf club, they would claim,
Was not to show off clothing but
To play to win the game.

Those dressed in showroom elegance
Had made the great mistake
Of leaving for the course just when
Their wife was wide awake.

She'd see what they were wearing and
She would have told them flat:
"Your trousers, shirt and socks don't match -
You can't go out like that."

"Whatever would the people think?
And I could get the blame;
To be seen dressed like that, it would
Besmirch the family name."

They wore what she suggested and
Gave thanks for her advice.
Their swing might be inhibited
But oh they did look nice!

PLAY IT AS IT LIES

One of the obvious rules of golf is that you play your next shot as the ball lies, without moving it to a more advantageous lie.

Some players that you might come across do not seem to fully understand this rule, and may need a gentlemanly reminder from time to time. The ball can, however, be moved with the agreement of those playing with you, or even against you, in a friendly game.

This may well apply where the ball lies in a scrape made by some wild animal. This rule is not supposed to apply to divots left by a wild golfer!

The ball may lie in a position such that to play it might cause damage to the player, his partners, or even the golf club being used to play the shot. In this situation, one might appeal to the generous nature of one's playing partners.

In some clubs there are 'winter rules' where, between certain winter dates, the ball can be moved to a preferred lie, but only on the fairway. This rule can be misinterpreted by golfers who do not refer to their calendars, or have a lapse of memory, or may be playing on a course that does not have winter rules, or, perhaps, invent winter rules of their own.

Play It As It Lies

The rules of golf are very clear,
With lies you cannot interfere;
Forget the wherefores and the whys,
We have to hit it as it lies.

Some balls hide where they won't be found,
They're almost buried in the ground;
Whatever spot it occupies,
We have to hit it as it lies.

And if anomalies appear,
The rules of golf will make it clear.
If there's not one that justifies,
We have to hit it as it lies.

I've played with golfers who don't get
The niceties of etiquette;
They tend to move the ball around,
As they would on the practice ground.

So when with strangers you might play,
Whose habits from golf rules could stray,
Agreeing early it might pay
To make strict rules apply that day.

GOLF BAGS

Golfers carry on to the course a golf bag which contains all they will need during the round.

Golf bags are designed to cater to all tastes, and come in all sizes, designs and colours.

The bags have slots for each of the clubs we are entitled to carry with us.

Most of us have favourite clubs, and clubs we rarely use because they don't work!

We possibly only need to carry the favourite ones, so could do with a much smaller 'practice bag'.

We do, however, carry the full set because we want any opponent to believe that we can hit them all! We bought them as a set and probably feel that if we left the odd one at home it would turn out to be the exact club we desperately needed for a particular shot during the round, when, of course, it would have worked beautifully.

I purchased a new golf bag recently that was ideal in every respect. It had plenty of storage pockets conveniently placed for all I needed to carry.

There was, however, one pocket near the top marked 'valuables'. This might be useful to any passing thief, but most golfers know where they secrete any valuables they might be carrying without drawing undue attention.

This labelling stood out because it was the only pocket that carried instructions for a particular use.

I have relabelled it 'the rules of golf' to emphasise the fact that I have studied and respect them. A hint, perhaps, that everybody should.

The following verse looks at a selection of items that are carried in golf bags by a variety of golfers.

Golf Bags

A golf bag should hold all we need,
Including special items we'd
Believed essential to our game;
But not all golfers think the same.

A set of golf clubs that we picked,
With style and balance that just clicked,
New golf balls, and a few we've found -
Enough to last us through the round.

Head-covers made in furry shapes
Like lions' heads, or dogs, or apes,
That friends and children bought for us
And we must use them without fuss.

The quantity of balls we take
Is sometimes hard to estimate.
Their number needs to near equate
To rotten shots, or whims of fate.

Golf tees of different heights and hues,
Are in our bag, and we all choose
The ones that suit us most to use,
In colours that are hard to lose.

A golf glove for the leading hand,
So perspiration will be banned
And we can keep an even grip,
So clubs within our hands won't slip.

Windcheater, for the wind that cuts
To keep us warm through drives to putts;
A discreet bottle that will hold
A tipple to keep out the cold?

And shaped containers some have got
To keep beer cool, when sun is hot;
And, wanting temperature precise,
There're some who'll even carry ice.

A golf hat tops the golf attire,
And some have style that all admire.
It shades the sunshine from our face
And keeps some errant hair in place.

Upon some golf hats you may find
Dark glasses, facing back behind.
The Pro, you'll find, will rarely play
With glasses worn the proper way.

A towel is an important touch
To clean golf balls and clubs and such
And, if we find an unsoiled spot,
Some perspiration we can blot.

Ball markers must be carried, too,
Although some golfers will make do
With coins that work quite well, we find,
But cost a bit if left behind.

We carry waterproofs around
In case of showers, but we've found
The time it takes to put them on,
That shower's very often gone.

An umbrella is a must,
For in our climate we don't trust
The whims of weather's moods unchecked,
That bring rain when we least expect.

Repairing pitch marks is a rule,
And for this job there is a tool.
And golfers all must carry one
To leave greens smooth when putting's done.

A distance finder's not a sin,
And tells us yardage to the pin;
Its better should the user know
How far each club they hit will go!

The 'rules of golf' must find a place
Within our golf bag, just in case
There is a query, and so you'll
Be able to explain the rule.

When travelling away from base,
The bag can be an extra case
To bring back items that you bought,
When cases full, and space is short.

ANIMALS ON GOLF COURSES

I was invited to make up a four-ball team when visiting a business conference in Cancun.

The course was beautiful, and our team was doing quite well, when we came to a par 3 of about 170 yards over a lake which had rough ground all around it.

My tee shot seemed good, cleared the lake but made an odd noise upon landing, and we all lost sight of it.

When we rounded the lake we saw why. It had obviously struck the 12ft alligator basking between the lake and the green.

My ball was lying midway between the two. Being aware that alligators can move at 40mph over short distances, and knowing that I can't, we discussed the pros and cons of moving the ball. As it seemed that, on that particular hole, my own score was important to the team's total, it was decided that I must play it as it lay.

I did so, but with great nervous apprehension. The alligator was quite unimpressed and did not move at all – I'm very glad to say.

On another occasion my wife and I attended a business convention at Sun City, the 'Las Vegas' of South Africa.

The resort had just been completed and was resplendent with its new championship golf course.

After getting the business part of the visit over, which didn't take very long, my host invited us to not only join him in a trip around the safari park, which was only a couple of miles away, but also, on the next day, to play a round of golf on the newly-opened Sun City course.

The safari park was large, hot, and full of mosquitoes, and we saw no wild animals, not even in the distance.

The next day some of us, accompanied by our wives, as team supporters, set out to play our much-anticipated round of golf.

We were approaching the green on a long par 4 when someone noticed that, on the fairway from which we had just played our approach shots, a large gathering of baboons had materialized. There was a large fierce-looking male, and his extended family.

Although we were all glad to see some wildlife at last, their proximity made some, especially the ladies, somewhat nervous.

Our host, with a seriously concerned look on his face, arranged for the ladies to stand in a semi-circle between the green and the baboons, and gave each a golf club for self-defence.

He told them to stand there and be ready to tell us if the baboons were attacking, while we putted out.

"If they do," he said, "Either run fast or use the club." He also added, "If the big one catches you it would be no use telling him you have a headache!"

After finishing the hole our host walked towards the baboons, clapped his hands, and they all ran off!

He was not popular and was almost the victim of an attack by the then-armed and very angry ladies.

Golf courses in all countries are homes to a variety of wild animals, small, large, or slithery, and we all learn to share the amenity with them.

Animals

Some courses lie, so lush and green,
On deserts' sandy flooring.
To play these courses can be fun
And very rarely boring.
The fairways end where desert starts,
With dangers at the edges;
The border's not protected by
Strong fences, walls or hedges.

These courses have clear signs that say
You must stay on the fairway,
For scorpions and rattlesnakes
Just want you out of their way.
Quite often you will see them where
Abandoned golf balls lie;
Collecting them is dangerous,
Unless you want to die.

In certain countries there are snakes
That you should not go near.
They may look pretty, but they are
The ones that you should fear.
When slithering across the course
They're easy to avoid,
But find them in the rough and you
Should not get them annoyed.

Now living in the UK we
Do not have vicious snakes;
Perhaps an adder could be found
Around some quiet lakes.
And grass snakes are quite plentiful
And often found in grass!
They are quite safe, and hide away
Where it is deep, not sparse.

Play golf in South America,
You might meet alligators,
And golfers who survive there do
Become good navigators.
While walking round the water's edge
Be careful if you've found them;
You can't tell if they're hungry, so
Just navigate around them.

And then some smaller animals
Know where they'll find a meal.
Its food that's left in buggies that
Those critters come to steal.
Some squirrels, monkeys, raccoons too,
Raid buggies, if they dare,
And other animals and birds
Join them and take their share.

They know the golfers' habits to
Bring food that they can munch,
In case their round is slow and they
Might be too late for lunch.
Because we don't use buggies in
The UK many times,
We don't have 'buggy followers',
Like those in warmer climes.

Some rabbits making scrapes that we
Might move our ball around,
Some pheasants walking proudly by,
And even deer are found.
But none take any notice of
Odd buggies they might meet,
For here our rounds are quicker
So we don't have time to eat.

And many other animals
Are seen around the world,
From warthogs through to kangaroos
Their species are unfurled.
Some wild cats have been seen around
And you might see them too,
Sometimes reports of larger ones
Escaping from some zoo.

But golf courses are very safe
For us to play our sport,
And dangers that you hear about
Most likely come to naught.
Perhaps the only dangers come
When playing with some fools
Who get you very angry when
They don't play by the rules.

BIRDS

When a young child is about to touch, or do, something they shouldn't, or something their mother disapproves of, she may say, "Ah-ah". This noise seems to stop the child, temporarily at least.

There is a bird that frequents courses in the south of America that makes a very similar sound.

A friend and I were visiting a course in South Carolina where he first encountered this bird call.

He was lining up his drive and was about to take his swing, when from somewhere came a clear "ah-ah".

He stopped, looked around feeling perhaps that someone wanted to criticise his stance and, when there was no further noise, he re-established his stance very carefully. Just before his swing, the "ah-ah" was repeated.

He looked around, puzzled and a little put out. “Don’t worry,” I said, “It’s only a local bird, and that’s probably its mating call”.

My friend took up his stance once more in fierce determination to get his drive away this time.

He took a wild swing, topped the ball, and it rolled only as far as the ladies’ tee.

From a nearby tree came, “Ah-ah, ah-ah, ah-ah, ah-ah.” We both fell about laughing, but I made him play the ball from where it lay. For a few holes he seemed to wait a bit before taking each swing, to allow for further ornithological criticism.

Birds

Apart from friendly ah-ah birds,
On open course, or heath,
There’re crows that pick up divots to
Find bugs that live beneath,
And birds so beautiful in flight
That we admire so much,
And little birds that flutter by,
And hawks, and doves, and such.

When playing in New Jersey once
We saw some vultures flying
In circles, in the distance, their
Sharp eyes we found were spying
A golfer who had given up,
For no more could he take.
They’d sensed his suicidal trend,
As he walked towards a lake.

We found the golfer later as
He sat beside the lake
Where he had thrown his bag of clubs,
His heart about to break.
We helped him haul his clubs back out
To play another day;
The disappointed vultures left
To look for other prey.

And there are birds of every type
On courses to be seen,
And golfers are at one with them -
They are part of the scene.
An eagle or an albatross
Is welcome any day -
We golfers are delighted if
One ever comes our way!

GOLF ON TV

Each evening, in the golfing season, television shows the action from the day's play in most tournaments.

As the bustle of the home dies towards bedtime, I am often left alone to watch my favourite sport.

I am accused of watching too much sport, but I explain that I am watching live drama yet to unfold, unlike the other TV dramas already in the can.

As I watch, I marvel at the skills that dedication and practice can create.

I wonder what I would have been like if I had concentrated on golf instead of all the other sports and pastimes and work that kept invading my life.

My daydreams are sometimes built around the possibility that I might even have been among those golfing warriors I am watching.

An idle thought, perhaps, but we can all have crazy dreams from time to time, even if we have to backdate them by scores of years.

Golf is now very well done on TV, and even the periods of televised sky, with a ball somewhere in it, can be exciting as we anticipate the quality of its landing.

Watching professional golf is always a lesson on how sport should be played without tantrums or arguments with those in authority. The rules are known and are followed.

Watching professionals play shots that we can only dream of, over lakes, around trees, from bunkers and sometimes from seemingly impossible lies, makes each moment exciting.

I will go on watching.

Golf on TV

When interviewed when round was done
About the shots they made,
The pros remember every one,
There were so few they played.

If asked about our own scores, we
Just haven't any hope -
When dealing with large numbers our
Own memories can't cope.

The pros hit balls that travel high,
Long airborne do they stay.
Perhaps it helps, they're playing on
A nice, warm, sunny day?

The commentators tell us that
An eight iron would be good;
The distance looked so great that we
Might well have used a wood.

Our expectations rising high,
We watch them putting out.
They miss a putt of thirty feet –
Their skills we start to doubt.

Then, if they hit a hook or shank
Our pride can swell a lot;
We're thinking, "Sometimes, even I
Could make a better shot."

That happens very rarely, so
On this we can't depend;
Our pride must go on making its
Excuses to the end.

And my excuse for watching golf,
My viewing in a groove?
I'm told that, if I watch enough,
My golf swing might improve.

But I enjoy the cut and thrust
Of dramas there to hand;
The instant, living scripts they write
With plots I understand.

EMOTION

A friend of mine and I had decided to enter a forthcoming competition as a pair. We therefore decided to play a round of golf together to discuss tactics.

My friend was a formidable man, with a voice to go with his size.

Unfortunately, we had chosen a very busy day on the golf course and most tee times had gone to a large group visiting from Japan.

We were fitted in between two visiting four-balls.

Waiting on a tee about midway through the round, we were looking down on the green from the previous hole, where four very serious-looking visitors were putting out.

We were watching one particular man stalking his five-foot putt. He circled it twice, looking at it carefully from front to back and from back to front, and from both sides.

He finally settled over his putt, played his shot and missed.

In a loud voice, in a language we did not know, he let out a tirade of emotional and fierce-sounding expletives.

My friend, in his not-too-quiet voice, said, "I wonder if that translates into '**Oh S...**'?"

The gentleman on the green heard him and turned to face us, bowed solemnly from the waist, and said, quite clearly, "Very similar, sir, very similar."

The joys and the emotions of this wonderful game are the same wherever it is played.

Golf stories and golf jokes are translated into many languages and are enjoyed around the world.

We meet people from all walks of life on golf courses, and our love for the game always seems to dominate over social divides, political affiliations, age differences and countries of domicile.

The game can be played seriously, with every shot counted and recorded, or can be played in a casual, friendly way, even allowing for slight adjustments to the lie of the ball in order to give the next shot a sporting chance. That only works if all players agree before the game starts.

Many more friendships are cultivated on the golf course than enemies ever made, even at highly emotional moments.

However, emotion and, perhaps, emotional outbursts, can play a great part in the game of golf and must be allowed to flourish, but always in such a way that would not unduly shock our mothers.

Emotion

That angry utterance we made,
Blood pressure going off the chart;
We'd hooked that shot we meant to fade,
Then our emotion played its part.

And, when we sank that eagle putt,
We gave way to unbridled glee.
We gave the air an uppercut -
Emotion showed for all to see.

Then when we topped that easy chip,
Repeated it, and gave a shout
Of anguish, let our language slip,
Emotion often breaks right out.

At last we've brought this game to heel,
The best score that we've shot for rounds,
Our happiness we can't conceal,
Emotion then can break its bounds.

This is a game of highs and lows,
The golfing spirits write the plot.
And then, whichever way it goes,
Emotion rides with every shot.

ETIQUETTE

There are conventional rules of social behaviour which apply to golf. Golf is a sport where sportsmanship reigns supreme and all who meet, and play the game, subscribe to this code of behaviour. Well almost!

Etiquette encourages us to follow the rules of golf to the letter, although there seem to be a few who don't know all the letters!

Anomalies can occur that seem to be outside the scope of the rules known by our playing partners, and these create healthy discussions in the bar after the round.

Most of the etiquette of golf seems to revolve around sportsmanship, fair play and a degree of logic.

Many golfers playing abroad take a copy of the *Royal & Ancient* rules of golf with them to settle any mild disputes.

Some even find that their lawyer makes a useful playing partner where heavy wagers are involved.

Etiquette

At all times our behaviour must
Conform to golfing etiquette.
Play fair, and in the rules we trust,
Our moral code with honour set.

We must not play our round too slow
And hold up those who're playing next,
Each waiting for their chance to go
And getting steadily more vexed.

And if we are behind slow play,
With patience just about to break,
Obscenities we mustn't shout
Or hit on through, or overtake.

We never make untimely noise,
To cough, or sneeze, or say a thing
That could affect a player's poise
While concentrating on their swing.

No form of 'sledging' is allowed,
Or any other harassment,
Or criticize another's shot,
Or laugh at their embarrassment.

However much we're tempted to,
We must not give or ask advice,
Except from playing partners, who
May not have answers that suffice.

We must count every shot we play,
Though we'll meet some who seem to score
Not counting 'air-shots' and the like,
Or shots they thought nobody saw.

With man-made objects such as walls,
Or buildings, that are in the way,
You're not allowed to move the ball,
Or buildings, just before you play.

We treat the course with great respect
And don't do damage, like a thug.
Repair our pitch marks on each green,
Replace all divots that we dug.

We will meet some, it's sad to tell,
Whose etiquette does not shine through.
They haven't learned the code too well,
But luckily they are but few.

REFLECTIONS IN THE BAR

A social drink in the club bar following a scintillating game of golf has, over the years, become almost traditional.

Groups chat together, often analyzing the highs and lows of the game just completed.

The reminiscences are very often full of 'if-onlys', and lapses of memory.

To hear some players talk, one would imagine that their round must have been near-perfect.

You knew it wasn't because it was you who was marking the card!

Of course it is understandable that people should mainly remember the best. Remembering the worst all the time is very negative and not good for us.

There seems to be an understanding that it would not be right to contradict some of these, often inaccurate, memories of the round.

Statements such as, "Wasn't that the hole you four-putted?" or, "It's a pity we couldn't find your ball on the third," should be resisted. Why make a player more demoralized than he already was by contradicting any positive memories he might have created?

To take some joy in a player's misfortunes should be a private emotion, un-displayed for anyone else to notice, unless he is your opponent actually during a match, when "Bad luck," or "Good try," or "I thought you'd sink that one," sincerely said, are usually sufficient to wind him up further.

Reflections in the Bar

I'm sitting in the clubhouse with
My second pint of beer,
Recalling how my round went, while
My memory's still clear.

Today's the day I could have played
Great golf right from the start;
My swing was near perfection, but
Misfortune played its part.

The sloping green upon the first
Needs back-spin with a wedge.
I hit it slightly thin and it
Went, first bounce, in the hedge.

Upon the next, that scream of "fore"
Caused my ungainly 'hack';
I'd tried to swing and duck at once
And nearly broke my back!

The wind was unpredictable,
It swirled around the course;
Behind, it was the lightest breeze,
In front, it was gale force!

The third requires a gentle draw,
With woodland down the right;
A rogue wind bent it toward those trees -
It ended out of sight.

The rough along the seventh hole
Was deep and thick and tall;
To dig it out you'd need a spade –
That's if you found the ball.

The short ninth hole looks easy
And my iron shot seemed grand,
But bounced upon a sprinkler-head
And ended in the sand.

The bunker on that 'easy' ninth
Plays well if ball lies true;
Except my ball lay in a print
Left by a size-twelve shoe!

My drive right down the par five tenth
Was poetry to see;
Its distance was prodigious, but
It stopped behind a tree.

My next shot was a beauty, but
It really was unfair;
Sir Henry Cotton wrongly preached
That trees were mostly air.

I could not, underneath that tree,
Improve my lie at all;
The rabbits had left many scrapes -
Not one was near my ball.

My drive way down the fourteenth was
Quite perfect, was it not?
But settled in a divot which
Destroyed my second shot.

Upon the green, my long, straight putt
Near left me quite bereft –
It bounced right off a bump just where
A pitch-mark had been left.

Some heavy rain engulfed me at
The far end of the course.
It soaked me to the skin, it came
With such torrential force.

The ants' nest that I stood upon
Just by the fifteenth green,
Has left my ankle with a rash,
The worst I've ever seen.

The itching of that poisonous rash
Now drives me round the bend.
It's spreading up my leg quite fast –
Don't know where it will end.

My drive upon the eighteenth hole
Was played in textbook style,
And, if it had not brushed that tree,
It would have gone a mile.

I grabbed my favourite iron,
Gave my second shot my all –
It soared into the stratosphere -
We never found the ball.

The bad luck that I've had this day
Is very hard to match;
With just a little better luck
I might have played to scratch!

But still it's been a good day, with
Great people I could share
The joys and the frustrations of
This game beyond compare.

FINAL THOUGHTS

I wish I could have brought golf more into my business life.

Over the years I have interviewed countless people for jobs in the organizations I have run.

Looking at their past history, listening to the answers to my questions and then having to make a decision based on an assessment of the person's character, can be somewhat hit-and-miss.

How much easier it could have been just playing a round of golf with them.

During 18 holes of golf you get to assess a person's character more completely than in any interview.

At whatever level their game might be, their true character will always shine through.

How they react to good luck, or a great shot; how they handle the 'slings and arrows of outrageous fortune'; how they get themselves together again after bad shots, and whether they tend to give up, or fight on with determination; where they place the blame for things that go wrong; how they keep their sense of humour in adversity; whether or not they show appreciation when others play good shots.

Do they, by any chance, help their score along by bending the rules a little, or failing to remember all the shots they played? Do they plan an attack on each hole, or just hit and hope?

These, and many other attitudes, actions and reactions would have given a clear indication of their strength of character and resilience. Of course, a chat in the bar afterwards might well complete the picture.

The theory works, but is impossible in practice because only a few of them will be golfers. More's the pity because, if there were more golfers, the world would be a much fairer and happier place.

We golfers should feel privileged to have the opportunity to play this fabulous game with like-minded people.

I wish you many happy hours on the golf courses of the world, striving for those odd moments of perfection that lie within all of us, and keep bringing us back.

OTHER BOOKS BY FREDDIE MITMAN

The Magic of Christmas Eve

A Christmas book, with illustrations, for both children and adults who believe in Father Christmas

Attitudes for Success

Learn the attitudes that bring success and give your own self esteem a boost.

9781784564315

ND - #0113 - 060826 - C86 - 210/148/5 - PB - 9781784564315 - Gloss Lamination